My Brother Lives in
Heaven

Written by
Tanya Hackett

Illustrated by
Maddy Moore

Briley & Baxter Publications | Plymouth, Massachusetts

Hardcover ISBN: 978-1-961978-29-4
Paperback ISBN: 978-1-961978-30-0

Book Design: Stacy A. Padula

Dedication

Jonny Hackett was an energetic 3.9 year-old little boy with intelligence that exceeded his years. He loved being outdoors, running, riding bikes, and cruising around on his four-wheeler. Jonny had a special relationship with his mama, and his daddy was his hero. His big brother, Bobby was his best friend. Jonny's adorable little smile and happy demeanor was enough to put a smile on anyone's face. Jonny left this world without a warning. On July 22, 2021, while swimming with his brother and friends, Jonny suffered an undetected ruptured brain aneurysm. Jonny fought hard but gained his wings on July 24th.

The Hacketts wanted to honor their son and help other families faced with tragedy. They started the Jonny Hackett Memorial Fund in October of 2021, and it has been a huge success. The fund provides "Jonny Bags" to local ICU's and emergency rooms. These bags are filled with items a family may need during an emergency or unplanned stay at the hospital. The Hacketts hope to keep their son's legacy going for years to come. This book is a continuum of that; they hope it will help other siblings and loved ones facing the loss of a special person. This book is dedicated to Jonny and the imprint he has left here on Earth.

My family may look like yours. I have a mom, a dad, and a little sister; but what you don't see is my little brother because he lives in *Heaven*.

Sometimes our loved ones leave us, which means we can't see them, hug them, or play with them anymore.

It's okay to be sad when someone goes to *Heaven*.
You will miss them, and it's okay to cry for them.
You cry for them because you love them.

In *Heaven*, our loved ones are met with beautiful angels, singing peaceful melodies. They are also reunited with loved ones who have already passed.

I envision *my brother* cruising on a quad through gold-covered streets. I can hear him giggling and laughing like we used to, overflowing with *joy* and *glee*.

I can see him living in the mansion *Jesus* prepared for him—the *Heavenly* home our family will one day live in together.

I can see him welcoming others into *Heaven*, like our dog Cam. I know they are playing frisbee and keeping each other company. They are so thankful to be together with *God* and the angels.

I like to think time stops in *Heaven*. Our loved ones who live there are not sad or scared. They are simply there watching over us, cheering us on, and waiting to be with us again.

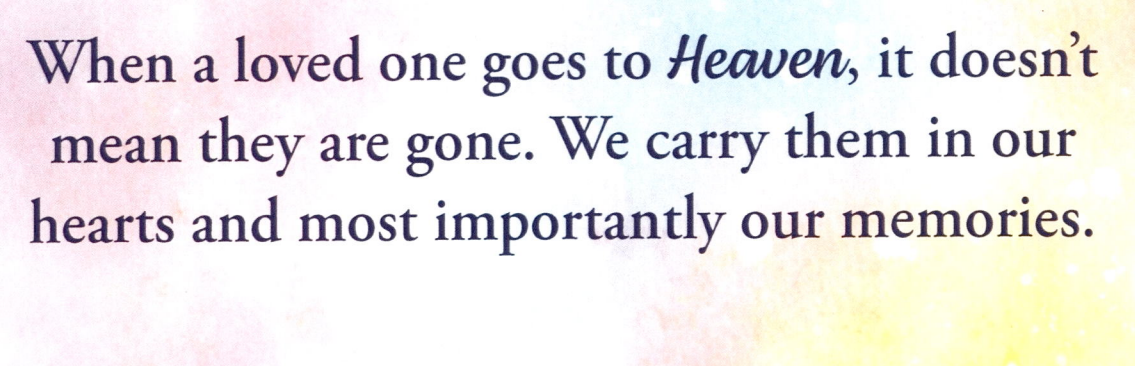

When a loved one goes to *Heaven*, it doesn't mean they are gone. We carry them in our hearts and most importantly our memories.

On special holidays, my family honors and remembers *my brother* by lighting a candle and sharing a silly memory of him.

We celebrate his birthday by sending a balloon into the sky with a message for him to catch while running through *Heaven's* beautiful fields of flowers.

Although we may have loved ones who are no longer here on Earth, *God* sends us signs so we know they are still with us.

My little brother will always be my brother; he just looks different to me now. I see him in the *rainbow* after every storm, the *dragonfly* flying over my head, and the *cardinal* sitting outside my window.

Whenever I see the signs, I always thank *God* and say hello to *my brother.*

I miss *my brother* very much, but I know he's always with me and that I will see him again one day.

When we are reunited, it will be for all *eternity* in a place where there is no pain, sickness, or sadness.

We will ride our quads down the gold-covered streets and giggle together.

We will *play* hide and seek, *dance* through fields of flowers, and *sit* under The Tree of Life.

We will feel like no time has passed.

Sometimes I still feel sad because I miss my brother being here. Sometimes I feel angry that he had to leave us so soon, but I know I have these feelings because *I love him* so much.

It's okay to be sad if your loved one now lives in *Heaven*, but remember to look for the signs from above.

Remember to share
memories and talk
about them with others
who miss them too.

I want to be with my brother, but I know I can't see him yet. I want to make him so proud as he cheers me on from *Heaven*. I have a lot I am meant to do before I can join him in eternity.

So, until then, I will look for the
rainbow, the dragon fly, and the
cardinal and know he is still with me.

About the Author

Tanya Hackett is the wife of a police officer and mother to three beautiful children: Bobby, Jonny, and Brooke. In 2015, Tanya began working as a social worker for the state of Massachusetts. Tanya's passion for helping others shined through her work with families and children in the community. It wasn't until the sudden, unexpected death of her son Jonny in 2021 that her mission shifted.

After losing her son, she was not only faced with her own grief, but also the grief of her son Bobby who was only five years old. Through her own blog and social media, she shared the rawness of the pain they felt and the pain of watching her son suffer with the loss of his little brother. Tanya realized this loss was not temporary and, in fact, is a life sentence of learning a new normal.

Tanya went on to dedicate her life to not only remembering and honoring her son through her foundation, but also normalizing grief and sharing her journey. This book is a look into what grief has been for her son Bobby, who is now turning eight years old. Tanya hopes this book will help other children who are suffering with an unimaginable loss.

Tanya plans to continue sharing this journey and hopes to someday write a follow-up book in the perspective of her daughter who was born a year after her brother Jonny gained his wings.

Jonny will always be a part of the Hackett family, and they will never stop sharing his legacy.

www.ingramcontent.com/pod-product-compliance
Lightning Source LLC
Chambersburg PA
CBRC100821120626
46547CB00010B/690